# 15-MINUTE STATIONS OF THE CROSS FOR KIDS

Meditations and Prayers for the Home, Church, or School

## JARED DEES

Illustrated by
**EZEKIEL SAUCEDO**

# TABLE OF CONTENTS

# INTRODUCTION

The Stations of the Cross, or Way of the Cross, is a wonderful devotion for children to have the opportunity to spiritually encounter Jesus Christ. There are so many great devotions in our Church's history, but this one appeals to children in many different ways.

Jesus said to his disciples, "If any want to become my followers, let them deny themselves and take up their cross daily and follow me" (Luke 9:23). Praying the Stations of the Cross allows children to accept this challenge. In understanding more deeply what it meant for Jesus to carry his cross, we can come to understand how we can carry ours.

## WHAT IS THE DEVOTION OF THE STATIONS OF THE CROSS?

The Stations of the Cross is a devotion to help us meditate on fourteen memorable moments of the passion and death of Jesus Christ.

The devotion has its origins in the city of Jerusalem, where Christian pilgrims would visit and walk along the same steps Jesus Christ walked on his way to his death. They would stop and recall specific moments of the passion and death of Jesus at fourteen specific places along the *Via Dolorosa*, which means "Way of Suffering."

Today those fourteen stations are also recreated with statues and religious images around the inside of Catholic churches. In addition, there are many examples of Stations of the Cross outside at various religious sites.

Especially during Lent but also at any other time during the year, people may pray at each one of the fourteen stations to remember the great sacrifice Jesus made for us on the cross. In this way, they can make a mini pilgrimage to Jerusalem and join in the journey of Christ's passion and death.

## THE FOURTEEN STATIONS OF THE CROSS

I. The First Station: Jesus Is Condemned to Death

II. The Second Station: Jesus Takes Up the Cross

## HOW TO PRAY THE STATIONS OF THE CROSS

The Way of the Cross is most often called the Stations of the Cross, because there are fourteen separate spots, or stations, that we travel to during the devotion. We begin at station one, usually marked with the Roman numeral I, and proceed to each of the fourteen stations to remember the events of Jesus's passion and death.

The traditional prayer we recite at each station is this:

*Leader: We adore you, O Christ, and we bless you.*

*All: Because by your holy cross you have redeemed the world.*

Alternatively, the leader will pray:

*We adore you, O Christ, and we praise you.*

To bless means to recognize God's presence here with us. To praise means to express how great someone is. We bless and praise Jesus Christ because of his great sacrifice for us.

Why was that sacrifice so great? Because through his suffering and death on the cross, he gained for us salvation. He freed us from the slavery of sin and opened up the gates of heaven for all who follow in his footsteps.

You can pray the Stations of the Cross alone or in groups. In a group setting there is usually a leader and a reader for each station, but everyone participates in reciting the traditional prayers. An illustration for each station is included with the meditations in this book for the times that you may want to pray the Way of the Cross outside of a church.

## MEDITATIONS FOR THE STATIONS OF THE CROSS

The purpose of Christian meditation is to enter into the mysteries of the life of Jesus Christ. This means to imagine ourselves in the stories of his life. By reading or listening to a meditation, we can reflect on how these moments have real-life applications for us today.

I wrote the meditations in this book after years of leading my students as a teacher and my children as a father through the Stations of the Cross. Each one of the different sets of meditations is meant to help kids connect their lives to the life of Christ on the cross.

## WHY FIFTEEN MINUTES?

As a teacher, I have seen the glazed-over eyes of my students as they listen to the long meditations and prayers at each station. I've even had students faint from the long moments of kneeling and standing.

As a dad I've done my best to keep my kids engaged while we join in the Stations of the Cross at home or in churches. It hasn't always been easy to keep them focused, especially when they were young.

The reality is that the attention spans of young people are surprisingly short. They maintain focus for a much shorter time than we think. It isn't their fault. I won't even blame the increase in technology and media. The fact is that kids are just kids. I wanted to create something that was respectful of their attention, with focused and relevant meditations that make them think.

I hope the kids who pray with this book will enjoy the Stations of the Cross as much as we do as adults. I hope that this will keep their attention on Christ and the life he wants to share with us. I hope these fifteen minutes of prayer will be a time to meet and grow in their relationship with Jesus Christ, who suffered, died, and redeemed the world.

## Part One

# THE FOURTEEN STATIONS OF THE CROSS

*Let the images alone guide you in this very simple Stations of the Cross for kids. Stop at each station and recite the traditional prayer and response. Pause and look at the images in this book or the statues or paintings of the stations in your church. Look at the art and let the Lord speak to you through the work of human hands.*

# I. THE FIRST STATION: JESUS IS CONDEMNED TO DEATH

**Leader:** We adore you, O Christ, and we bless you.

**All:** Because by your holy cross you have redeemed the world.

# II. THE SECOND STATION: JESUS TAKES UP THE CROSS

**Leader:** We adore you, O Christ, and we bless you.

**All:** Because by your holy cross you have redeemed the world.

# III. THE THIRD STATION: JESUS FALLS THE FIRST TIME

**Leader:** We adore you, O Christ, and we bless you.

**All:** Because by your holy cross you have redeemed the world.

# IV. THE FOURTH STATION: JESUS MEETS HIS MOTHER

**Leader:** We adore you, O Christ, and we bless you.

**All:** Because by your holy cross you have redeemed the world.

# V. THE FIFTH STATION: SIMON OF CYRENE HELPS JESUS CARRY THE CROSS

**Leader:** We adore you, O Christ, and we bless you.

**All:** Because by your holy cross you have redeemed the world.

# VI. THE SIXTH STATION: VERONICA WIPES THE FACE OF JESUS

**Leader:** We adore you, O Christ, and we bless you.

**All:** Because by your holy cross you have redeemed the world.

# VII. THE SEVENTH STATION: JESUS FALLS THE SECOND TIME

**Leader:** We adore you, O Christ, and we bless you.

**All:** Because by your holy cross you have redeemed the world.

# VIII. THE EIGHTH STATION: JESUS MEETS THE WOMEN OF JERUSALEM

**Leader:** We adore you, O Christ, and we bless you.

**All:** Because by your holy cross you have redeemed the world.

# IX. THE NINTH STATION: JESUS FALLS THE THIRD TIME

**Leader:** We adore you, O Christ, and we bless you.

**All:** Because by your holy cross you have redeemed the world.

# X. THE TENTH STATION: JESUS IS STRIPPED OF HIS GARMENTS

**Leader:** We adore you, O Christ, and we bless you.

**All:** Because by your holy cross you have redeemed the world.

# XI. THE ELEVENTH STATION: JESUS IS NAILED TO THE CROSS

**Leader:** We adore you, O Christ, and we bless you.

**All:** Because by your holy cross you have redeemed the world.

# XII. THE TWELFTH STATION: JESUS DIES ON THE CROSS

**Leader:** We adore you, O Christ, and we bless you.

**All:** Because by your holy cross you have redeemed the world.

# XIII. THE THIRTEENTH STATION: JESUS'S BODY IS TAKEN DOWN FROM THE CROSS

**Leader:** We adore you, O Christ, and we bless you.

**All:** Because by your holy cross you have redeemed the world.

# XIV. THE FOURTEENTH STATION: JESUS IS LAID IN THE TOMB

**Leader:** We adore you, O Christ, and we bless you.

**All:** Because by your holy cross you have redeemed the world.

# A FIVE-MINUTE STATIONS OF THE CROSS FOR KIDS

*Here are fourteen meditative prayers for children and teens to recite as they move through the Stations of the Cross. Invite them to make these prayers their own as they look to Jesus and reflect on their lives. Each station and prayer should take only 20–30 seconds to complete.*

## I. THE FIRST STATION: JESUS IS CONDEMNED TO DEATH

**Leader:** We adore you, O Christ, and we bless you.

**All:** Because by your holy cross you have redeemed the world.

**Reader:** Jesus, you were punished for a crime you didn't commit. You were innocent, but I am guilty every day of making mistakes. That is why you died for me. Thank you for being punished so that I can go to heaven without being punished.

**All:** Amen.

## II. THE SECOND STATION: JESUS TAKES UP THE CROSS

**Leader:** We adore you, O Christ, and we bless you.

**All:** Because by your holy cross you have redeemed the world.

**Reader:** Jesus, you carried the cross and you didn't complain. It is easy for me to find things to complain about. Give me the strength to do hard things without complaining, just like you.

**All:** Amen.

## III. THE THIRD STATION: JESUS FALLS THE FIRST TIME

**Leader:** We adore you, O Christ, and we bless you.

**All:** Because by your holy cross you have redeemed the world.

**Reader:** Jesus, you fell but you got back up again. Give me the strength to get up when I fall down. Give me the courage to do things that are important but hard for me to do.

**All:** Amen.

## IV. THE FOURTH STATION: JESUS MEETS HIS MOTHER

**Leader:** We adore you, O Christ, and we bless you.

**All:** Because by your holy cross you have redeemed the world.

**Reader:** Jesus, you loved your mother so much. I love my parents, too. Thank you for the gift of their love.

**All:** Amen.

## V. THE FIFTH STATION: SIMON OF CYRENE HELPS JESUS CARRY THE CROSS

**Leader:** We adore you, O Christ, and we bless you.

**All:** Because by your holy cross you have redeemed the world.

**Reader:** Jesus, you let Simon help you carry the cross. Show me how I can help you today and throughout my life. I want to serve you. Give me the strength to help.

**All:** Amen.

## VI. THE SIXTH STATION: VERONICA WIPES THE FACE OF JESUS

**Leader:** We adore you, O Christ, and we bless you.

**All:** Because by your holy cross you have redeemed the world.

**Reader:** Jesus, you welcomed Veronica's help as well. Thank you for all the people you have put into my life to help me: family, friends, teachers, coaches, priests, and more.

**All:** Amen.

## VII. THE SEVENTH STATION: JESUS FALLS THE SECOND TIME

**Leader:** We adore you, O Christ, and we bless you.

**All:** Because by your holy cross you have redeemed the world.

**Reader:** Jesus, you fell again and no one was there to pick you up. Forgive me for the times I didn't help those in need. Give me the ability to be generous toward others who need my help.

**All:** Amen.

## VIII. THE EIGHTH STATION: JESUS MEETS THE WOMEN OF JERUSALEM

**Leader:** We adore you, O Christ, and we bless you.

**All:** Because by your holy cross you have redeemed the world.

**Reader:** Jesus, you met the women of Jerusalem, who were crying as they watched you suffer. When I see someone upset, help me comfort them.

**All:** Amen.

## IX. THE NINTH STATION: JESUS FALLS THE THIRD TIME

**Leader:** We adore you, O Christ, and we bless you.

**All:** Because by your holy cross you have redeemed the world.

**Reader:** Jesus, you fell a third time, but you didn't give up. The next time I want to quit or say "I can't" do something, give me the confidence to finish what I started.

**All:** Amen.

## X. THE TENTH STATION: JESUS IS STRIPPED OF HIS GARMENTS

**Leader:** We adore you, O Christ, and we bless you.

**All:** Because by your holy cross you have redeemed the world.

**Reader:** Jesus, they took everything away from you, even your clothes. I have a lot of clothing and possessions that are very important to me. Help me to love you above all things and be ready to give up everything to follow you.

**All:** Amen.

## XI. THE ELEVENTH STATION: JESUS IS NAILED TO THE CROSS

**Leader:** We adore you, O Christ, and we bless you.

**All:** Because by your holy cross you have redeemed the world.

**Reader:** Jesus, I can only imagine how painful it must have been for you to die on the cross. Thank you for making such a great sacrifice for your people. I will never forget what a great gift it was for me.

**All:** Amen.

## XII. THE TWELFTH STATION: JESUS DIES ON THE CROSS

**Leader:** We adore you, O Christ, and we bless you.

**All:** Because by your holy cross you have redeemed the world.

**Reader:** Jesus, your death makes me sad, but I know why it was so important. You died so that when I die, I can join you in heaven. There is nothing I could ever do to thank you enough for this great gift. Thank you, Jesus. Thank you.

**All:** Amen.

## XIII. THE THIRTEENTH STATION: JESUS'S BODY IS TAKEN DOWN FROM THE CROSS

**Leader:** We adore you, O Christ, and we bless you.

**All:** Because by your holy cross you have redeemed the world.

**Reader:** Jesus, they took down your body from the cross, and your mother was there to receive you. My family is there for me. My friends are there for me, too. Thank you for their love and care.

**All:** Amen.

## XIV. THE FOURTEENTH STATION: JESUS IS LAID IN THE TOMB

**Leader:** We adore you, O Christ, and we bless you.

**All:** Because by your holy cross you have redeemed the world.

**Reader:** Jesus, they laid your body in a tomb and rolled a stone to cover up the opening. Your body was there all alone. I sometimes feel alone, but I know you are always with me. Thank you for your daily presence in my life.

**All:** Amen.

## Part Three

# A FAMILY STATIONS OF THE CROSS FOR KIDS

*These fourteen meditations can be used by individual families or in a group of families. The meditations and prayers ask kids and parents to reflect on family life and to pray with thanksgiving and petitions to the crucified Lord to bestow his blessings upon us.*

## I. THE FIRST STATION: JESUS IS CONDEMNED TO DEATH

**Leader:** We adore you, O Christ, and we bless you.

**All:** Because by your holy cross you have redeemed the world.

**Reader:** Parents sometimes have to punish their children or correct them when they do something wrong.

Can you think of the last time your parents punished you?

[Pause for twenty seconds of reflection]

Jesus was punished, too. He was sent to his death for a crime he didn't commit.

He was innocent, but he died for us.

**All:** Lord, thank you for your great sacrifice for us.

## II. THE SECOND STATION: JESUS TAKES UP THE CROSS

**Leader:** We adore you, O Christ, and we bless you.

**All:** Because by your holy cross you have redeemed the world.

**Reader:** We see crosses all over our churches and homes today.

Think about where you see crosses in your home or church. Picture them in your mind.

[Pause for twenty seconds of reflection]

Today it is easy to forget how embarrassing it was to be killed on a cross in the ancient world.

Crucifixion was the most shameful way to be killed in the Roman Empire.

But Jesus wasn't embarrassed by the cross.

We aren't embarrassed either. The next time you look at the cross, remember what Jesus did for us.

**All:** Lord, we are proud to be your servants.

## III. THE THIRD STATION: JESUS FALLS THE FIRST TIME

**Leader:** We adore you, O Christ, and we bless you.

**All:** Because by your holy cross you have redeemed the world.

**Reader:** When children fall, they either get up on their own or a grown-up picks them up to make sure they are okay.

Can you think of a recent cut, bruise, or injury you had? Was anyone there to make sure you were okay?

[Pause for twenty seconds of reflection]

Jesus fell, but he got back up again on his own.

He was on a mission to make sure we would be okay for eternity.

**All:** Lord, thank you for taking care of the souls of our family.

## IV. THE FOURTH STATION: JESUS MEETS HIS MOTHER

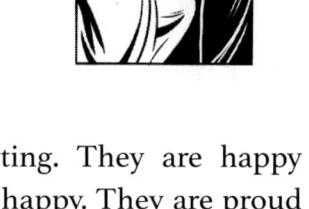

**Leader:** We adore you, O Christ, and we bless you.

**All:** Because by your holy cross you have redeemed the world.

**Reader:** Parents love their children. They hurt when they see their children hurting. They are happy when they see their children happy. They are proud when they see their kids do well.

Think about a recent moment of joy you had with your mom or dad.

[Pause for twenty seconds of reflection]

We have to wonder what Mary felt, seeing her son suffer and die on the cross. Was she sad, or was she proud of him?

Probably both, as well as so many more emotions, because she loved him with all her heart.

**All:** Lord, help us to love our parents as much as you loved your mother.

## V. THE FIFTH STATION: SIMON OF CYRENE HELPS JESUS CARRY THE CROSS

**Leader:** We adore you, O Christ, and we bless you.

**All:** Because by your holy cross you have redeemed the world.

**Reader:** A man named Simon carried the cross for Jesus for a short distance.

What are some ways you have helped your siblings or parents recently?

[Pause for twenty seconds of reflection]

Sometimes, like Simon, we have the opportunity to help people in need. This can require us to sacrifice our time, our energy, and our own wishes to do something else.

Jesus needs our help. He needs us to do hard things to help others in need, just as Simon helped him carry the cross.

**All:** Lord, give me the strength to help others when they need it most.

## VI. THE SIXTH STATION: VERONICA WIPES THE FACE OF JESUS

**Leader:** We adore you, O Christ, and we bless you.

**All:** Because by your holy cross you have redeemed the world.

**Reader:** Jesus carried the cross with a crown of thorns on his head. Veronica saw that his face was dripping with sweat and blood, so she wiped his face for him.

What are some ways you can help your parents even before they ask for help? For example, what could you clean up in the house for them?

[Pause for twenty seconds of reflection]

No one needed to tell Veronica to help. She saw Jesus suffering, and she did the right thing.

**All:** Lord, forgive me for the times I haven't helped when I could.

## VII. THE SEVENTH STATION: JESUS FALLS THE SECOND TIME

**Leader:** We adore you, O Christ, and we bless you.

**All:** Because by your holy cross you have redeemed the world.

**Reader:** Carrying the cross took a while. Jesus fell more than once. The Roman soldiers must have been impatient and annoyed with his falls.

Is there anything members of your family do that annoys you?

[Pause for twenty seconds of reflection]

Your family's annoying habits are opportunities to avoid anger. They are opportunities to remember Jesus falling.

Rather than becoming angry with someone for falling, be merciful, as God is merciful to you.

**All:** Lord, give me the patience to accept the annoying things my family does around me.

## VIII. THE EIGHTH STATION: JESUS MEETS THE WOMEN OF JERUSALEM

**Leader:** We adore you, O Christ, and we bless you.

**All:** Because by your holy cross you have redeemed the world.

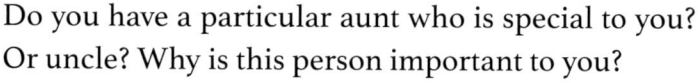

**Reader:** A group of women from Jerusalem watched and wept for Jesus as he carried the cross. They were sad to see him suffer.

Do you have a particular aunt who is special to you? Or uncle? Why is this person important to you?

[Pause for twenty seconds of reflection]

We have many people outside of our immediate family who care about us and cry for us when we are hurt or unhappy.

Jesus told the women of Jerusalem not to cry for him, but he didn't send them away.

**All:** Lord, thank you for the people outside of our immediate family who love and care about us.

## IX. THE NINTH STATION: JESUS FALLS THE THIRD TIME

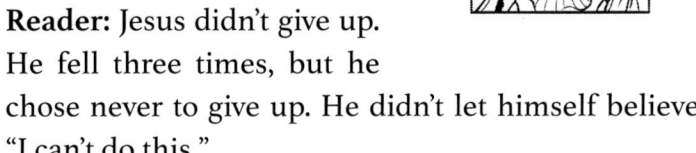

**Leader:** We adore you, O Christ, and we bless you.

**All:** Because by your holy cross you have redeemed the world.

**Reader:** Jesus didn't give up. He fell three times, but he chose never to give up. He didn't let himself believe "I can't do this."

When have you wanted to give up? When have you thought you couldn't do something?

[Pause for twenty seconds of reflection]

As a family, we give each other moral support. We help each other believe we can do things even when we want to give up.

Don't give up. Jesus didn't give up, because he knew that his passion and death were too important.

**All:** Lord, thank you for your great courage. Help me to believe in myself as strongly as you believe in me.

## X. THE TENTH STATION: JESUS IS STRIPPED OF HIS GARMENTS

**Leader:** We adore you, O Christ, and we bless you.

**All:** Because by your holy cross you have redeemed the world.

**Reader:** The Roman soldiers stripped Jesus of the only thing he had left: his clothes.

What are some of your favorite clothes? Did you buy them for yourself, or did your parents pick them out? Did your siblings help?

[Pause for twenty seconds of reflection]

Sometimes we pick clothes for practical reasons, like staying cool or staying warm.

Other times we pick clothes because of the way they make us look. Jesus wore very simple clothing, but even that was taken away from him. He had nothing left by the time he died.

He gave it all up for you.

**All:** Lord, help me to think less about how I look and more about how you look at me.

# XI. THE ELEVENTH STATION: JESUS IS NAILED TO THE CROSS

**Leader:** We adore you, O Christ, and we bless you.

**All:** Because by your holy cross you have redeemed the world.

**Reader:** The Roman soldiers nailed Jesus's hands and feet to the cross and raised him up for all to see.

When was the last time someone in your family said something to you that hurt your feelings?

[Pause for twenty seconds of reflection]

People will hurt us, either on purpose or by accident. It is natural to be upset and angry, but don't let the anger overwhelm you.

Imagine the pain Jesus experienced when his hands and feet were nailed to the cross.

Don't forget what he said about the people who hurt him: "Father, forgive them. They know not what they do."

**All:** Lord, forgive us for hurting each other's feelings, and help us to forgive others when they hurt us.

# XII. THE TWELFTH STATION: JESUS DIES ON THE CROSS

**Leader:** We adore you, O Christ, and we bless you.

**All:** Because by your holy cross you have redeemed the world.

**Reader:** Jesus Christ, the Son of God, died for us.

God sent his only Son, Jesus, to die for us.

What are some of your parents' greatest sacrifices for you?

[Pause for twenty seconds of reflection]

Parents love their children more than anything in the world.

God loved his child more than any one thing in the world, but he gave Jesus up for the whole world.

God the Father let Jesus suffer because he loves us. Jesus the Son suffered and died because he loves us.

What else can we do but adore God?

**All:** Lord, thank you for sending your Only Begotten Son to suffer and die for our family.

## XIII. THE THIRTEENTH STATION: JESUS'S BODY IS TAKEN DOWN FROM THE CROSS

**Leader:** We adore you, O Christ, and we bless you.

**All:** Because by your holy cross you have redeemed the world.

**Reader:** Jesus's mother, Mary, was there to receive his body as it was taken down from the cross.

When was the last time you felt your mother's embrace? Or your grandmother's hug?

[Pause for twenty seconds of reflection]

Mothers carry their children in the womb. They give birth to us all. They love us throughout our whole lives.

Mary had this same unique love for the Son of God. Moments earlier, Jesus told her from the cross to look upon his disciple as her son. He told his disciple to look upon Mary as his mother.

The Virgin Mary, Mother of God, looks down on us now with the love of a mother for her children.

**All:** Lord, thank you for giving us your mother to love and pray for us and our greatest needs.

## XIV. THE FOURTEENTH STATION: JESUS IS LAID IN THE TOMB

**Leader:** We adore you, O Christ, and we bless you.

**All:** Because by your holy cross you have redeemed the world.

**Reader:** After all the pain and suffering, there is now silence. Jesus has died, but the story is not over.

Have your parents ever made you end a game or stop watching a show or movie before it was over? What does that feel like?

[Pause for twenty seconds of reflection]

While the Stations of the Cross might end here, the story is not over.

After the silence of the tomb will come the great joy of the Resurrection.

But for now, we wait to see the ending, just like turning off a game or movie before it is finished.

**All:** Lord, give me the patience to get through difficult times and know that joy is on the way.

## Part Four

# A SCHOOL STATIONS OF THE CROSS
# FOR KIDS

*This collection of meditations was written for all-school assemblies in Catholic schools and parish religious education programs, or for anyone to lead children in a set of reflections specifically focused on school life. Kids spend the majority of their days in school, and these meditations will help them reflect on their educational experience as it relates to the passion and death of Christ.*

# I. THE FIRST STATION: JESUS IS CONDEMNED TO DEATH

**Leader:** We adore you, O Christ, and we bless you.

**All:** Because by your holy cross you have redeemed the world.

**Reader:** Detention is the classic form of punishment in schools. Traditionally, kids sit in a room quietly after school until the detention time is over. Jesus's punishment was so much worse than a detention. He suffered incredible pain and was killed, all for a crime he didn't commit.

Think of the last time you got into trouble or made a mistake at school. What were the consequences?

[Pause for twenty seconds of reflection]

Jesus's crucifixion was like a friend who did nothing wrong serving someone else's detention time without asking anything in return. He was punished and died so we wouldn't have to die and suffer for eternity.

**All:** Lord, thank you for the great gift of your life for us.

# II. THE SECOND STATION: JESUS TAKES UP THE CROSS

**Leader:** We adore you, O Christ, and we bless you.

**All:** Because by your holy cross you have redeemed the world.

**Reader:** As students, we raise our hands when we know the answer. Sometimes, though, we get the answer wrong. This can be embarrassing.

When was the last time you felt embarrassed in school?

[Pause for twenty seconds of reflection]

The cross was the greatest embarrassment of ancient times. People were crucified to bring shame upon them for their crimes. Jesus wasn't embarrassed. He embraced the cross and accepted his mission.

He was beaten and laughed at. The soldiers placed a crown of thorns on his head to mock him. He didn't complain, and he didn't get embarrassed. He maintained confidence in the cross.

**All:** Lord, give me the courage to overcome embarrassment as you did on the cross.

## III. THE THIRD STATION: JESUS FALLS THE FIRST TIME

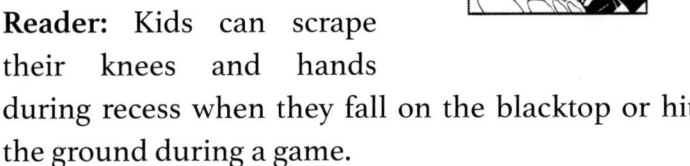

**Leader:** We adore you, O Christ, and we bless you.

**All:** Because by your holy cross you have redeemed the world.

**Reader:** Kids can scrape their knees and hands during recess when they fall on the blacktop or hit the ground during a game.

How well do you handle pain when you fall? Do you stay tough or cry a little when you get hurt?

[Pause for twenty seconds of reflection]

Jesus fell during the Crucifixion many times. He was hurt, but he didn't cry or complain. He got back up again because he knew he was suffering that pain for you.

**All:** Lord, give me the strength to overcome my greatest pains.

# IV. THE FOURTH STATION: JESUS MEETS HIS MOTHER

**Leader:** We adore you, O Christ, and we bless you.

**All:** Because by your holy cross you have redeemed the world.

**Reader:** Parents sometimes come to school to take their kids home when they are feeling sick.

When was the last time your parents came to your school? What was it like to see them in the school building?

[Pause for twenty seconds of reflection]

Unlike a parent coming to take their sick kids home from school, there was nothing Mary could do to help Jesus.

She had always been there for him, from laying him in a manger to the Crucifixion. Now there was nothing she could do to help other than let him know how much she still loved him.

**All:** Lord, help us to love you as much as Mary loved your Son.

## V. THE FIFTH STATION: SIMON OF CYRENE HELPS JESUS CARRY THE CROSS

**Leader:** We adore you, O Christ, and we bless you.

**All:** Because by your holy cross you have redeemed the world.

**Reader:** Teachers often ask students to work in pairs or groups on assignments. Partners and group members help each other out during these projects.

What has been your favorite group project in school?

[Pause for twenty seconds of reflection]

The Romans assigned Simon of Cyrene to help Jesus carry the cross for a short time.

We are assigned to help Jesus carry the cross as well. We do this by the way we offer up a little suffering in service to others.

Just as each partner in a project needs to do their best to help, we need to do our best to help Jesus.

**All:** Lord, I will serve you and do what is right to help others in need.

# VI. THE SIXTH STATION: VERONICA WIPES THE FACE OF JESUS

**Leader:** We adore you, O Christ, and we bless you.

**All:** Because by your holy cross you have redeemed the world.

**Reader:** There are many opportunities for students to share during school. We can help a classmate who needs a pencil, pen, or paper. We can invite someone to join in a conversation in the hall or a game during recess.

When was the last time someone shared with you at school or invited you to join them in a game or group?

[Pause for twenty seconds of reflection]

Veronica saw Jesus suffering, and she helped him. She shared a cloth to wipe his sweaty and bloody face.

No one asked her to help. She didn't care that the cloth would be ruined. Jesus needed help, and she helped him.

**All:** Lord, help us to see the needs of those around us and share generously with those who need it.

## VII. THE SEVENTH STATION: JESUS FALLS THE SECOND TIME

**Leader:** We adore you, O Christ, and we bless you.

**All:** Because by your holy cross you have redeemed the world.

**Reader:** All kids struggle in school at one time or another. Some struggle more than others, but everyone makes mistakes.

How do you react when someone makes a mistake in class? Can you think of a time when your classmates laughed at someone's mistake or laughed at you?

[Pause for twenty seconds of reflection]

Some people laughed at Jesus when he fell.

Our God knows what it is like to fall. He knows what it feels like for others to laugh at you when you are down.

We can always turn to him when we make mistakes, and we can always help others when they fall.

**All:** Lord, be my strength when I make mistakes, and help me when I fall.

# VIII. THE EIGHTH STATION: JESUS MEETS THE WOMEN OF JERUSALEM

**Leader:** We adore you, O Christ, and we bless you.

**All:** Because by your holy cross you have redeemed the world.

**Reader:** Many kids dislike public speaking. It can be scary to read or present in front of the class.

When was the last time you stood up to read or present in front of the class? Did you like it or not?

[Pause for twenty seconds of reflection]

Jesus had a crowd of people watching him. The women of the city of Jerusalem were crying as they watched him carry the cross.

Jesus didn't want their pity. He didn't want their attention. He wanted them to pause and reflect on their own lives.

We can do the same. Pause and reflect on your own life and relationship with God today.

**All:** Lord, open my heart and mind to understand your will for my life today.

## IX. THE NINTH STATION: JESUS FALLS THE THIRD TIME

**Leader:** We adore you, O Christ, and we bless you.

**All:** Because by your holy cross you have redeemed the world.

**Reader:** Some things in school are really difficult to understand. Your hardest subject might be math or English or history or maybe even PE or art.

Have you ever had such a hard time learning something that you wanted to quit? When was the last time you wished you could skip a subject in school?

[Pause for twenty seconds of reflection]

Jesus fell three times on the Way of the Cross, but he didn't quit. He got back up again each time and kept going.

When you feel like quitting, remember Jesus carrying the cross. He did not quit.

Keep going. Everyone falls and wants to give up. Keep trying, and eventually you will get it.

**All:** Lord, give me the strength to get up when I fall and keep going when I want to quit.

# X. THE TENTH STATION: JESUS IS STRIPPED OF HIS GARMENTS

**Leader:** We adore you, O Christ, and we bless you.

**All:** Because by your holy cross you have redeemed the world.

**Reader:** Many kids worry about what they will wear to school. They worry about what people will think of them. They try to dress in a way that will make people like them.

What is your favorite outfit to wear to school? Why do you like it so much?

[Pause for twenty seconds of reflection]

The Roman soldiers took everything away from Jesus, even his clothes. He had nothing left. There was no way to hide. Yet people still loved him. We have statues of Jesus nearly naked and hanging on the cross, yet we still love and respect him. The less we worry about our clothing, the more open we are to the love that God has for us. He loves us no matter what we wear. That love is all that matters.

**All:** Lord, thank you for the love you have for me no matter what I look like or what I wear.

# XI. THE ELEVENTH STATION: JESUS IS NAILED TO THE CROSS

**Leader:** We adore you, O Christ, and we bless you.

**All:** Because by your holy cross you have redeemed the world.

**Reader:** When kids bring home their report cards, their parents get to see how well they are doing in class.

How did you do on your last report card? What did your parents think or say about it?

[Pause for twenty seconds of reflection]

Jesus dedicated his life to serving his people. He healed, preached, and taught them everything they needed to know to find a happy life.

When you get good grades, your parents and teachers praise you. Jesus should have received glory and praise at the end of his life, but instead he was nailed to the cross to die a horrible death.

He suffered that pain for you and me. He didn't seek glory or praise. He sought to serve and ignored the negative criticism of others.

**All:** Lord, thank you for giving up your life for me.

## XII. THE TWELFTH STATION: JESUS DIES ON THE CROSS

**Leader:** We adore you, O Christ, and we bless you.

**All:** Because by your holy cross you have redeemed the world.

**Reader:** Jesus Christ is with you at every moment of the day.

How often do you turn to him during school? Do you ask for help in doing well? Do you ask for forgiveness for mistakes? Do you ask for strength when you struggle? Do you give thanks when things are good?

[Pause for twenty seconds of reflection]

Jesus Christ died on the cross, but he rose again. He ascended into heaven, and now he is spiritually by our side every single moment of the day.

Never forget him. Always turn to him throughout the day, even in school.

**All:** Lord, thank you for your loving presence throughout each day.

# XIII. THE THIRTEENTH STATION: JESUS'S BODY IS TAKEN DOWN FROM THE CROSS

**Leader:** We adore you, O Christ, and we bless you.

**All:** Because by your holy cross you have redeemed the world.

**Reader:** Sometimes kids can't wait for the bell to ring to mark the end of class or the end of the school day.

The class or day often ends with joy for what's next.

Do you look forward to the bell ringing? Why or why not?

[Pause for twenty seconds of reflection]

The end of Jesus's life was not a moment of joy. As they brought his body down from the cross, there was sadness and weeping.

Thankfully, the story was not over. Joy was coming soon. Jesus died, but he would rise again.

The sadness of death is followed by the joy of the Resurrection.

**All:** Lord, give me a happy ending to this day, with joyful anticipation for the happy days ahead.

# XIV. THE FOURTEENTH STATION: JESUS IS LAID IN THE TOMB

**Leader:** We adore you, O Christ, and we bless you.

**All:** Because by your holy cross you have redeemed the world.

**Reader:** It is often difficult for kids to sleep on the night before the first day of school or the night before a big school event.

When was the last time you couldn't sleep because you were thinking about the next day?

[Pause for twenty seconds of reflection]

They laid Jesus's body in a tomb and all was silent. Now the waiting began. As the story of the cross comes to an end, a new day is about to begin. Jesus will rise and the waiting will be over. Joy is on the horizon!

**All:** Lord, take away my worries about the future and fill me with the calm joy of your Resurrection.

## Part Five

# A VIRTUES STATIONS OF THE CROSS FOR KIDS

*The seven Catholic virtues include both the theological virtues and the cardinal virtues. The theological virtues are the gifts of faith, hope, and charity. The cardinal virtues are prudence, temperance, justice, and fortitude. There are two meditations on each of the virtues throughout these fourteen Stations of the Cross. The first seven meditations ask you to reflect on your past experiences of the virtues, and the last seven meditations will help you practice them in the future.*

## I. THE FIRST STATION: JESUS IS CONDEMNED TO DEATH

**Leader:** We adore you, O Christ, and we bless you.

**All:** Because by your holy cross you have redeemed the world.

### Justice

**Reader:** We meditate on the virtue of justice, which means fairness. Jesus was unfairly sent to his death, and no one tried to stop it.

Who do you know of today that is being treated unfairly?

**All:** Lord, help me bring justice to those who are treated unfairly.

## II. THE SECOND STATION: JESUS TAKES UP THE CROSS

**Leader:** We adore you, O Christ, and we bless you.

**All:** Because by your holy cross you have redeemed the world.

### Hope

**Reader:** We meditate on the virtue of hope, which is trust in God. The soldiers laid the cross on Jesus's shoulders. His future was hopeless. He was sure to die. The people witnessing these events were surely without hope at the time.

When have you experienced a hard and hopeless time in your life?

**All:** Lord, give me hope when times are hard.

## III. THE THIRD STATION: JESUS FALLS THE FIRST TIME

**Leader:** We adore you, O Christ, and we bless you.

**All:** Because by your holy cross you have redeemed the world.

### Fortitude

**Reader:** We meditate on the virtue of fortitude, which means courage. It took tremendous courage for Jesus to die for us. He must have used every bit of his strength to carry the cross, but he did not give up. He kept going no matter how hard it was for him.

When have you needed fortitude to do something that was very difficult for you?

**All:** Lord, give me the fortitude to do challenging things even when I am afraid to fail.

## IV. THE FOURTH STATION: JESUS MEETS HIS MOTHER

**Leader:** We adore you, O Christ, and we bless you.

**All:** Because by your holy cross you have redeemed the world.

### Charity

**Reader:** We meditate on the virtue of charity, which means selfless love. Mary's love for her son was self-less because she did not stand in the way of his suffering and death. She knew the reason for his sacrifice and set aside her own pain as she watched him on the way to his death.

When have you set aside what you wanted in order to help someone else get what they wanted or needed?

**All:** Lord, let your love for Mary fill me with the charity to help others most in need today.

## V. THE FIFTH STATION: SIMON OF CYRENE HELPS JESUS CARRY THE CROSS

**Leader:** We adore you, O Christ, and we bless you.

**All:** Because by your holy cross you have redeemed the world.

### Prudence

**Reader:** We meditate on the virtue of prudence, which means wisdom. Simon helped Jesus carry the cross. He didn't deny this opportunity or run away. He chose to help Jesus. It was a wise choice that can inspire us to do the same.

When have you been faced with a difficult decision?

**All:** Lord, give me the prudence to make wise choices to help you and others who are most in need.

## VI. THE SIXTH STATION: VERONICA WIPES THE FACE OF JESUS

**Leader:** We adore you, O Christ, and we bless you.

**All:** Because by your holy cross you have redeemed the world.

### Faith

**Reader:** We meditate on the virtue of faith, which means belief in God. Many people watched Jesus suffer and die, but only a few believed he was truly the Messiah. Veronica saw Jesus for who he really was and maintained her belief in him no matter what it cost.

What helps you maintain your belief in God?

**All:** Lord, give me faith to believe in you even when others doubt your power.

## VII. THE SEVENTH STATION: JESUS FALLS THE SECOND TIME

**Leader:** We adore you, O Christ, and we bless you.

**All:** Because by your holy cross you have redeemed the world.

### Temperance

**Reader:** We meditate on the virtue of temperance, which means self-control. Jesus did not lose his temper with the soldiers who led him to his death. Even when they mocked him and spat on him, he controlled his emotions. He maintained focus on a much more important goal.

When have you struggled to be patient and in control of your emotions?

**All:** Lord, give me the temperance to be patient when I want to be angry or annoyed.

## VIII. THE EIGHTH STATION: JESUS MEETS THE WOMEN OF JERUSALEM

**Leader:** We adore you, O Christ, and we bless you.

**All:** Because by your holy cross you have redeemed the world.

### Prudence

**Reader:** We meditate on the virtue of prudence. When Jesus saw the women of Jerusalem crying for him, he told them to cry for themselves. Sometimes we need to look inward to find the right ways to react to situations.

When is the best time of day for you to reflect on how prudent you have been in the choices you make?

**All:** Lord, help me to see the ways I can be more prudent throughout my day.

# IX. THE NINTH STATION: JESUS FALLS THE THIRD TIME

**Leader:** We adore you, O Christ, and we bless you.

**All:** Because by your holy cross you have redeemed the world.

## Justice

**Reader:** We meditate on the virtue of justice. Jesus knows what it is like to fall. He knows what it is like to be treated poorly and oppressed. There are many people in the world today who need us to pursue justice on their behalf to help them get back up again.

How can you help bring about justice for the poor and vulnerable in the world today?

**All:** Lord, help me always pursue justice for the poor and oppressed.

## X. THE TENTH STATION: JESUS IS STRIPPED OF HIS GARMENTS

**Leader:** We adore you, O Christ, and we bless you.

**All:** Because by your holy cross you have redeemed the world.

### Temperance

**Reader:** We meditate on the virtue of temperance. The Roman soldiers divided Jesus's garments among themselves by throwing dice. They made it into a game. There are times when we will be tempted to choose fun over what is most important.

When are you most likely to be tempted to choose fun over responsibility?

**All:** Lord, help me to practice temperance when I am tempted to have too much fun and ignore what or who is most important in each moment.

## XI. THE ELEVENTH STATION: JESUS IS NAILED TO THE CROSS

**Leader:** We adore you, O Christ, and we bless you.

**All:** Because by your holy cross you have redeemed the world.

### Fortitude

**Reader:** We meditate on the virtue of fortitude. Each moment of Jesus's suffering and death seemed to be more painful than the last. Yet he maintained his strength through the pain. We all need the strength to resist pain and not complain when things are difficult.

What can you do instead of complaining about things in your life?

**All:** Lord, give me the fortitude to fight through pain without complaining.

## XII. THE TWELFTH STATION: JESUS DIES ON THE CROSS

**Leader:** We adore you, O Christ, and we bless you.

**All:** Because by your holy cross you have redeemed the world.

### Charity

**Reader:** We meditate on the virtue of charity. Jesus's death was the ultimate act of loving charity. He gave up everything for us. Meanwhile, we often struggle to share some of the simplest things in our lives.

When can you be more selfless and share what you have with others?

**All:** Lord, inspire in me a love and desire to share with others no matter how much I want to keep something for myself.

## XIII. THE THIRTEENTH STATION: JESUS'S BODY IS TAKEN DOWN FROM THE CROSS

**Leader:** We adore you, O Christ, and we bless you.

**All:** Because by your holy cross you have redeemed the world.

### Faith

**Reader:** We meditate on the virtue of faith. Jesus's death was a great test of faith for the disciples. Their master was gone. They were all alone, and all they could do was wait and see if what he had predicted would come true. We will all be tested in our faith at one time or another. For this we must be prepared.

What can you do to strengthen your faith in God on a daily basis?

**All:** Lord, increase my faith to overcome any test of my trust in you.

## XIV. THE FOURTEENTH STATION: JESUS IS LAID IN THE TOMB

**Leader:** We adore you, O Christ, and we bless you.

**All:** Because by your holy cross you have redeemed the world.

### Hope

**Reader:** We meditate on the virtue of hope. Jesus's body was laid in a dark tomb with a stone rolled across the entrance. The disciples could no longer see him. They could only wait in silent hope for the return of their Lord. We cannot see God today, yet we must maintain our hope in him no matter how bad things seem to be for us.

How can you comfort others who need more hope in their lives?

**All:** Lord, help me to be a beacon of hope for others when they need it the most.

# ABOUT THE AUTHOR

Jared Dees is the creator of The Religion Teacher (TheReligionTeacher.com), a popular website that provides practical resources and teaching strategies to religious educators. A respected graduate of the Alliance for Catholic Education (ACE) program at the University of Notre Dame, Dees holds master's degrees in education and theology, both from Notre Dame. He frequently gives keynotes and leads workshops at conferences, church events, and school in-services throughout the year on a variety of topics. He lives near South Bend, Indiana, with his wife and children.

Learn more about Jared's books, speaking events, and other projects at jareddees.com.

# ALSO BY JARED DEES

Jared Dees is the author of numerous books, including a short story collection titled *Beatitales: 80 Fables about the Beatitudes for Children*.

Download a collection of these stories at jareddees.com/beatitales.

## BOOKS BY JARED DEES

*31 Days to Becoming a Better Religious Educator*

*To Heal, Proclaim, and Teach*

*Praying the Angelus*

*Christ in the Classroom*

*Beatitales*

*Tales of the Ten Commandments*

*Do Not Be Afraid*

*Take and Eat*

*Pray without Ceasing*

*Take Up Your Cross*

*Prepare the Way*

*Advent with the Angels*

# ABOUT THE ILLUSTRATOR

Ezekiel Saucedo is an author and illustrator from San Antonio, Texas. His first graphic novel, *Saint John the Baptist: A Voice Crying Out in the Desert*—published by Pauline Books & Media—is the culmination of a lifelong passion for artistic interpretation and innovative storytelling. He looks forward to continuing to share the stories of our Catholic tradition through engaging narratives and vibrant artwork.

You can follow his work at zekesaucedo.com.

Made in United States
Cleveland, OH
31 August 2025

19873112R10066